Some Things Are Priceless

Some Things Are Priceless

Laura Lee Oldham

ABINGDON
Nashville

Some Things Are Priceless
Copyright © 1981 by Abingdon

Library of Congress Cataloging in Publication Data

Oldham, Laura Lee, 1931-
   Some things are priceless.
    1. Family—Religious life—Meditations.   2. Oldham, Laura Lee, 1931-
I. Title.
BV4526.2.042   242'.64   81-3498   AACR2

ISBN 0-687-39060-5

Scripture quotations unless otherwise noted are from the King James
Version. Quotations noted TLB are from *The Living Bible*, copyright © 1971
Tyndale House Publishers, Wheaton, Illinois. Used by permission. Quota-
tions noted NAS are from the New American Standard © The Lockman
Foundation; 1960, 1962, 1963, 1968, 1971, 1972. World Publishing, Times
Mirror, N.Y. Quotations noted NAVES are from Nave's Topical Bible, a
Digest of the Holy Scriptures, Topical Bible Publishing Company. Quotation
noted Williams is from *The New Testament: A Translation in the Language of the
People* by Charles B. Williams. Copyright © 1937 by Bruce Humphries, Inc.
Copyright © renewed 1965 by Edith S. Williams. Used by permission of
Moody Bible Institute.

Picture credits: pages 13, 117 by Anthony Black, Lynchburg, VA; pages 27,
73, 107, 127 by Doug Oldham; page 39 by Rebekah Oldham; page 65, Bracey
Holt; page 87, Janet Ross Photograph, Cincinnati Zoo; page 97 by Sue
Buchanan.

The prayer on page 64 is from *The Authorized Daily Prayerbook* by Dr. Joseph
Hertz. Copyright © 1948, 1975 by Ruth Hecht, New York, N.Y. Sixteenth
printing, 1979. Used by permission.

Lines quoted on page 124 are from "I Could Never Outlove the Lord" by
William J. and Gloria Gaither. © Copyright 1972 by William J. Gaither. All
rights reserved. International copyright secured. Used by permission of the
Benson Company, Inc., Nashville.

A special thanks to Elaine Evans for typing this manuscript, and more
importantly, for "laughing at life" with me for twenty years.

Book Design by Laura Wooten

Manufactured by the Parthenon Press at
Nashville, Tennessee, United States of America

This book is dedicated to Doug
who took a girl from the homestead,
set out to show her the world,
treat her like a queen,
and entertain her as if she were a
whole star-studded audience.
He has succeeded
to the highest possible degree,
in all three!

May all husbands everywhere
go and do likewise.

CONTENTS

BROTHER MOTHER

As Jesus was speaking in a crowded house his mother and brothers were outside, wanting to talk with him. When someone told him they were there, he remarked, "Who is my mother? Who are my brothers?" He pointed to his disciples. "Look!" he said, "these are my mother and brothers." Then he added, "Anyone who obeys my Father in heaven is my brother, sister and mother!" Matthew 12:46-50 (TLB)

My family calls me "Brother Mother" at home. Paula, our oldest daughter, started it. It's a joke. You know how kids are about parents. I never gave it any serious thought, but even so, it always pleased me, way down deep. Then one day, thinking about it, and about this book I was trying to write, I remarked to Doug, "Maybe we should call the book 'Brother Mother.'" We both laughed and forgot it. Forgot, that is until the next time I picked up my Bible, and those very words in scripture jumped out at me from Matthew 12. (As you can see, we ended up calling the book something else.)

So there it is. That funny little family, who so love to laugh at my eccentricities and foibles, had just unwittingly paid me a very fine compliment. Luckily they consider me not merely a natural, earthly mother, but one with them in their daily struggle of learning how to be a Christian. We are, after all, just learners together, each trying our best to follow the better, higher road of life. It's the road where Jesus walked, long ago, and still is walking, urging us to climb along with him.

My husband, children, mother, in-laws, sons-in-law, and one brother and sister-in-law are all on that same road.

What is my motive in bringing into print a book?

If it's true that we are all one another's mother, sister, brother, then it behooves me to share everything I am and have to encourage each family member.

And who is my family?

"Anyone who obeys my Father in heaven is my brother, sister and mother!"

"I know you well; you aren't strong, but you have tried to obey and have not denied my Name. Therefore I have opened a door to you that no one can shut." Revelation 3:8 (TLB)

One night we had a young friend in for dinner. He was desperately lonely. His lovely young career-oriented wife had decided it was better for her career not to be married and had filed for divorce. He was devastated! So were we, as we listened. Here was divorce, a closed door, a locked door, with someone throwing away the key.

Reading this scripture from Revelation the next morning after the dinner, I began to think about that "open door." Divorce is a closed door. Marriage is like an open door.

Stepping across the threshold of that open door come friends, family, in-laws, newborn babies, other people's children, people carrying in groceries for a party, someone bringing a fresh-cut fragrant bouquet of flowers. Dogs and cats scamper across to play. Presents and gifts are carried across to convey what the heart wants to say. Christmas trees get dragged across and Easter baskets smuggled in. People with sorrows come for comfort. Children with hurts come for handouts. Teen-agers with longings come for counsel. The aged grandparents come for love and care, and grandbabies come to bake cookies. The line of people is endless.

What is marriage? Two people in tune with each other and their world. And they become a wonderful, welcoming open door.

For He has clothed me with garments of salvation,
He has wrapped me with a robe of righteousness,
As a bridegroom decks himself with a garland,
And as a bride adorns herself with her jewels. . . .
So the Lord God will cause righteousness and praise
To spring up before all nations.   Isaiah 61:10b, 11b (NAS)

I didn't like it much, but it was cheap. It had been on display in the window and it *was* a satin wedding dress, and it *did* fit. So I put a little money down and promised to bring along fifty more dollars . . . somehow. My in-laws-to-be were graciously paying for the church wedding, but I did feel obligated to at least buy the gown. In a couple of weeks a cashier's check made out to me for fifty dollars arrived in the college mail! It would buy the dress! Who had sent it? I knew not, but guessed it might be the friend who was to be our best man.

After the wedding, the dress was boxed and moved with all our other things so many times, I lost track of it. It had served its purpose and didn't seem to be of any special value.

Then one day a few weeks before her wedding, Paula, our oldest daughter, came sailing down the stairs with the wedding dress on, laughing and dancing and saying to her excited sisters and girl friend, "Oh, I found it! I love it! I'm going to wear it for my wedding!" I was aghast! "Why? That's a terrible wedding dress. I never liked it."

"Oh, no it's not!" she said. "It's beautiful and I'm going to wear it!" And she did!

It looked beautiful and she was beautiful! We purchased a lovely lace veil to go with it. One that the saleslady would hardly sell us. "It was out of style," she said, "and no one would want it." It was also cheap. But we loved it and we wanted it. After the wedding the dress got packed away with a great deal more care.

Then before long, Karen was to be married. "I'll wear the dress too, Momma, and I'll wear Paula's veil! I love it. It will be so beautiful!" So a friend made a trip to Chicago and bought some fabulous imported lace that looked like the lace on the veil. She cut out lace flowers and appliquéd them all over the soft, old satin dress. It was suddenly lovely enough to be in a museum. So Karen wore my dress and her sister's veil. She looked so gorgeous when she came down the aisle, I thought my heart would stop!

And there was *that* dress that I didn't like and had bought cheap and hauled around not paying it any mind, considering it worthless. There was *that* dress looking for all the world like a royal robe fit for a queen! What of its value now? Priceless. Absolutely priceless . . . not because of the material, the satin, the lace, or the style. Priceless because of the human values . . . two lovely daughters had loved me enough to want to wear my dress . . . because our own marriage had almost failed, but didn't. It came back with great love and beauty . . .

because of two more young marriages doing well . . . and because my father-in-law, the girls' grandfather, said the vows for us all—all in the same dress.

Those are the reasons why a piece of satin and lace can be called priceless!

By the way, remember the cashier's check that paid for the dress in the first place? I just found out a few years ago, twenty-five years after the wedding, that it came from my husband.

Priceless? Yes. Some things are priceless.

"Sir, which is the most important command in the laws of Moses?"

Jesus replied, " 'Love the Lord your God with all your heart, soul, and mind.' This is the first and greatest commandment. The second most important is similar: 'Love your neighbor as much as you love yourself.' All the other commandments and all the demands of the prophets stem from these two laws and are fulfilled if you obey them." *Matthew 22:36-40a (TLB)*

I watched my four-year-old granddaughter Jamaica trying to help one-year-old Baby John walk the other day. He still approaches the feat like a tightrope walker, throwing little arms to the side, trying to get and keep his balance. Whenever he fell, Jamaica would try to pick him up. Sometimes she didn't lift enough and they both fell in a heap. Sometimes she lifted too much and pulled his feet off the floor, overbalancing them both, and down they would go again. He didn't like her help and sent up a howl.

"That's a picture of me trying to be a mother," I thought. Sometimes, I didn't lift enough in my children's development and we all fell. Sometimes, I lifted too much and again we fell back instead of growing.

The intent of Jamaica's heart is right. She wants John to walk and walk well, not losing his balance. In her awkward way, she's trying to help. Like Jamaica, I've had the right motives. I've wanted my children to live, and live right, not losing their balance.

In my awkward way, I've tried to help. Baby John won't

hold it against Jamaica that her help wasn't perfect. I hope my girls won't hold it against me that mine has been imperfect.

I learned the hard lesson a few years ago that it's destructive to hold it against my parents and my husband's parents, that they lifted too little or too much with us.

Maybe it's a good place to start this book, forgiving our imperfect families for their awkward help and like Baby John does Jamaica, love her for her love and for trying!

Behold, how good and how pleasant it is for brethren to
dwell together in unity!   Psalm 133:1

On one of Doug's tours, we were driving through the
Garden Spot of America, the beautiful San Joaquin Valley of
California, and as the bus topped a rise in the road, those
aboard looked out on a gorgeous, huge, well-cared-for truck
farm. In the garden was a family of five people holding
hands—mother, father, and three children. The strange thing
was, they had birds sitting all over them! A closer look
revealed that the family was a family of scarecrows put up to
scare the birds away from the vegetables.

Why weren't the birds scared? I don't know.

I suspect it has something to do with the fact that the
scarecrows were a family.

A family is a disarming unit. A family disarms fear. Five
people holding hands and happily making their way through
each day encounter far fewer fears than one person fighting the
battles alone.

Birds are smart. One scarecrow with clothes flapping in the
wind could give a bird a fright. But a family?

P-shaw!

SET AT NOUGHT

And Herod with his men of war set him at nought, and mocked him, and arrayed him in a gorgeous robe, and sent him again to Pilate.   Luke 23:11

The phrase "set him at nought" means literally to make him seem as if he were nothing, thus Herod unwittingly taught us a great lesson. Our attitudes toward others determine whether they appear to be "something"—or whether they appear to be "nothing."

Parents can make a child that is "really something" appear to be "practically nothing."

Christians can hold an attitude toward other Christians that make them appear as nothing.

Husbands and wives can nothing out or cancel out each other's positive potentials and traits.

Someone has said, "Act as if—and you will become." This certainly seems to be true. Whatever we act as if the people around us are, that is what they will become.

It behooves us, therefore, to set about acting as if those closest to us are valuable persons—intricate, unique, special somebodies. Likewise, we can see our fellow Christians as the true gems of this world—special souls called of and accepted by God.

Most of all, I want to view Jesus, as Jesus, the very Christ, the one who is all, the beginning and the end. May nothing in my attitude toward him ever be guilty of setting him at nought—making him seem as nothing.

"Heaven can be entered only through the narrow gate! The highway to hell is broad, and its gate is wide enough for all the multitudes who choose its easy way. But the Gateway to Life is small, and the road is narrow, and only a few ever find it."   Matthew 7:13-14 (TLB)

Twice before we had climbed this high mountain. To make the climb, we drive almost to the top, and then finish by climbing the rest on foot.

Mt. Evans in Colorado has the highest mountain road in the United States, and nobody doubts this claim once they've made it to the top. Near the top is the shelter house which is literally built into the rocks for safety from the high winds. Most people stop there, sip hot tea, and enjoy homemade doughnuts while marveling at the view. But the brave souls don jackets and climb the rocky trail to the peak.

The Mt. Evans trip has always been a thrill, but this particular day I was very excited. John, our son-in-law, loves a map. The family has had many friendly arguments over his continual map reading. But this day, because of John and his map, I discovered something truly amazing. I found my home-land—where I grew up. There it was, maybe a hundred miles away. John, with map unfurled, was pointing to landmarks that I remembered! There was the big high plain with what we called "the Hog's Back" curving through it, and there was the South Platte River. It was all spread out before us like a living map. I was so thrilled I could hardly stand it!

Finally, as we started down the mountain we suddenly saw

something else to astound us—an apparition rose through the mist of distance. A great argument ensued. John's map was consulted, and sure enough, we were seeing the skyscrapers of Denver, looking for all the world like an ethereal city come down from heaven surrounded by swirling clouds.

In another time, another place, another John *did* see the Holy City come down from the heavens.

Twice before we had been up the mountain, but without John and his map, we didn't know we were looking at my beloved homeland or the mile-high city.

John and his map can be translated into a Christian and his Bible. We need to keep checking our map! If we don't, we may not know where we are, or we may have the homeland in view and not recognize the landmarks. We might even miss seeing the glory of the Holy City altogether!

Both the map and the Bible are at times a little hard to read, but it's always worth the effort to find out where we are, where we are going, and what we've seen.

John and his maps! He can make a believer out of you!

"So whose wife will she be in the resurrection? For she was the wife of all seven of them!"
But Jesus said, "Your error is caused by your ignorance of the Scriptures and of God's power! For in the resurrection there is no marriage; everyone is as the angels in heaven." Matthew 22:28-30 (TLB)

This isn't a very popular message. It's easy to see why. First of all, our greatest insults on earth are leveled at animals or people we consider neuter. We love being male and female!

Second, if we do have a wonderful, loving marriage, we don't want to think that someday the relationship will be null and void. Even if we try to foresee that it might be better, it's hard to imagine.

I don't want to give the devil any credit here, but I'd still like to say he seems to think because this physical part of our lives doesn't go with us into heaven, he has special rights in this area. He's wrong, but he does take some ungodly liberties with us all, and causes some real battles.

In trying to get our spiritual perspective, I think it's important to remember that sexual love is part of our physical bodies. It will not last beyond the grave. But there is a new love—a love we can never know here, that will make all our love relationships complete and joyous. It's wonderful, and beyond our knowing!

Now, is all of this discussion of any earthly good here and now? Maybe. Today, if I have a disagreement with Doug, my husband, and am hopping mad at him, I can take the sting out

23

of it. All I need do is remember that someday, he won't be a husband . . . he'll be "as an angel"! (I can just imagine him with Triple-X size wings!)

He'll be complete in the Lord, as I'll be complete in the Lord, as all love will be complete.

Think what a relief that will be!

Look upon mine affliction and my pain; and forgive all my sins. Psalm 25:18

Long ago my little child came to me in tears and said, "Mother, you told me not to touch your favorite vase, but I did and I broke it. Mother, I'm so sorry, please forgive me; and look I have cut my hand!"

She took care of what was most important first by asking for my forgiveness and receiving my love, before she remembered her physical hurt and said, "Look at the cut."

That was the wonderful wisdom of a child, in realizing what was most important—asking forgiveness—and what was secondary—asking for help with the pain.

I should be so wise when going to my heavenly Parent. I do want him to "look at my pain." I want my physical illness to be subjected to his loving mercy. But most of all, I want his forgiveness and love for any intentional or unintentional breaking of his "favorite vase," his law.

Praise ye the Lord. O give thanks unto the Lord; for he is good: for his mercy endureth for ever. Psalm 106:1

 TREES

I will instruct thee and teach thee in the way which thou
shalt go: I will guide thee with mine eye.   Psalm 32:8

Some beautiful trees in view from our kitchen window are towering cedars, surely planted when the house was built, 130 years ago. An ancient oak down in the meadow is silhouetted against rolling hills and sky. There are also a black walnut and a fruit-bearing plum. All are beautiful, all symmetrical, each distinctive, each different from all the others. Good planning, God's planning, went into those trees. I appreciate them.

However, if I left my kitchen and climbed one of those trees to sit up among the branches, I would surely have a different view of them. Those branches would appear to be going every which way. I wouldn't be able to see much of a plan, if I were in the middle of the leaves and branches.

For today, I'm going to have faith to believe that life is like that. We're each viewing our own lives from the middle of our own tree. It looks pretty confusing. But God, the planner, steps back and views the life in perspective, seeing its beauty, symmetry, and individuality.

He did the planning and the planting. All I'm doing is growing in his care—trusting his design.

"He will not be disheartened or crushed,
Until He has established justice in the earth;
And the coastlands will wait expectantly for His
law."   Isaiah 42:4 (NAS)

John Claypool in his book *Tracks of a Fellow Struggler* uses the term "the language of events." When I came across that phrase, it caught me up short. There it was—the description, in four simple words, of how we figure out the Lord's working in our lives!

I have been *reading* events, as a book from the Lord, all my life. Many times the book was too deep for me, and I didn't understand, but that didn't stop the reading. Like any book, that can't be read before it has been written, so we can't read the events of life before they happen. We live life, then we read those events and see what the Lord is saying to us. By the direction those events have taken, we can usually get some idea which way the Lord is leading. But by not being able to read ahead, or to read the last page first, we are kept from getting cocky or sure of ourselves.

Life is forever the greatest of mystery stories. The solution is always out ahead in the next to the last page.

THE EVENING LIGHT

And the city had no need of the sun, neither of the moon, to shine in it: for the glory of God did lighten it, and the Lamb is the light thereof.   Revelation 21:23

There is an "evening light" that has intrigued me for many years, that comes just before dark. It isn't the sun, for the sun is down. Rather, it is a special glow that nestles close to the ground, and lasts only for a few minutes. It is as if the soil, the grass, the shrubs, and the small trees have absorbed light from the sun and are aglow with a golden inner light. It is so unearthly and beautiful, I always watch for it in the evening. It reminds me of those childish toys that absorb light when children hold them near the light, and glow when they sneak them under the covers after they go to bed. It is magical.

Some day, all we who are called by his name will live in a wondrous city. The city will need no sun, no moon, no electricity, no street lights, no gas lights. The light in this perfect city will be the Lamb of God, Jesus, the very one who was crucified for us. He who is our spiritual light here on earth will be our actual light in that city, and the glory of God will be over all.

Maybe the unusual evening light we see here is but a momentary flash of light from that city, like the northern lights are flashes of electrically charged particles from the sun.

There are wonderful things that we know not of—in that heavenly land where the Lamb is the light.

Doth not wisdom cry? and understanding put forth her voice? She standeth in the top of high places, by the way in the places of the paths. She crieth at the gates, at the entry of the city, at the coming in at the doors. Unto you, O men, I call; and my voice is to the sons of man.   Proverbs 8:1-4

Wisdom, in the form of the Spirit of God, does seek us out, even children, wherever we may be. I've been watching for a long time now to see if this is true, and I'm convinced that it is.

Somewhere between two and four, I encountered this Spirit of Wisdom. I was a little mountain girl, living in a remote log cabin in the Rocky Mountains with wonderful, gentle parents and a grand older brother. There were no churches, no Sunday schools, no phonograph records. I even remember when our first radio came in the mail. There was no talk of God that I can recall. This is not to discredit my family—I just wasn't aware of any talk, if it was there.

Sitting in the old rope swing one day, kicking dry dust with tan bare feet, I watched the white fleecy clouds float across the blue sky and got lost in my imagination. There was "Someone wonderful up there," I just knew it! And he loved me! I sent back a soundless message that I loved him, too.

This ethereal experience, even though childish, was dramatic and made a lifetime impression on me. I hinge the whole bent of my life's longings on that one moment. Henceforth I wanted to be good and in tune with that wonderful Spirit Person.

As a mother, I also watched my own little girls, usually around age four, experience some "moment of truth," some encounter with that beautiful Spirit of Wisdom. And they all responded positively. This is not to say they were saved. They were *bent*, or called or chosen. God did not leave them untouched as children.

I thank him that he reaches and touches and pulls, even in the streets where his name is not heard. If we learn to encourage when we see he has left his mark on a heart, we'll be workers with him.

GRANDPA BROWN

I have been young and now I am old. And in all my years I
have never seen the Lord forsake a man who loves him; nor
have I seen the children of the godly go hungry.
                                    Psalm 37:25 (TLB)

   Grandpa Arthur Leakey Brown is now a hundred years old.
He always said he wanted to live to be one hundred. Well, he
made it. President Carter sent his greetings and MacDonald's
(as in hamburgers) gave him a big party.
   Grandpa makes us laugh! All the things that his one hundred years of living encompass are phenomenal. We've been
saving his letters for the past twenty years, thinking each one
might be the last letter. He's outlived several specially purchased "burial suits." They're now motheaten and outmoded.
Ah, well, still he lives!
   He isn't a perfect man, this ancient shoe cobbler. He was an
orphan and suffered many longings because of it. He wasn't a
perfect father and caused his children some sufferings. But he
kept trying, and finally when he was quite old, he reached the
point where he completely gave himself to the Lord. His
shortcomings began to recede and a sweetness surfaced.
   His later years have been lovely. He is hard to care for
physically, but his spirit is a joy to others. He wakes up each
morning singing and he loves everyone. And he suffers no
pain—much to his doctors' and nurses' amazement. On his one
hundredth birthday, they were discussing this unusual state,
and one of the nurses finally summed up her thoughts by

saying, "Maybe God is trying to show us, those who care for Gramps, that he, the heavenly Father, does care for his own in special and marvelous ways."

She must be right. Grandpa Brown's life is making a grand statement, straight from the Bible: "God cares for his own!"

Then Jesus called the children over to him and said to the disciples, "Let the little children come to me! Never send them away! For the Kingdom of God belongs to men who have hearts as trusting as these little children's. And anyone who doesn't have their kind of faith will never get within the Kingdom's gates."   Luke 18:16-17 (TLB)

I just paid a week-long visit to a nursing home. My mother is there. Such a visit makes me agonize and cry and suffer and worry—and laugh. Persons could get well-nigh hysterical if they drew parallels between old age and childhood.

Children go through a stage of learning to walk in a walker. Oldsters get to the stage of *keeping* walking with a walker. All two-wheeled vehicles need a third wheel added for youngsters. It is also back to the three-wheeled bike for the oldsters.

Children are messy eaters and need little bibs. Same story way down the years.

Troubles with the potty plague the child. You guessed it.

Children's storybooks have big print and simple stories. Same goes for the grandmothers.

When music hour comes for the child, out come the rhythm instruments—sticks and bells and triangle. For the old? Yep.

It's wonderful, it's terrible, it's grand, it's sad. It may also be necessary in God's scheme. He said, "Except ye be converted, and become as little children, ye shall not enter into the kingdom of heaven" (Matt. 18:3). We've always preached that to mean that we should be like a child in simple trust and eager love, while we're still in command of our lives. But perhaps God allows old age to happen to us, so our earthly props of sophistication and power and intellect and prestige all come to nothing and we are again little children, in body as well as in spirit, totally dependent upon his care and keeping.

There is something lovely here—in spite of everything. The body deteriorates, so the spirit can learn to live—in another dimension, another place, another time—with the Guardian of all the ages as parent!

I will be your God through all your lifetime, yes, even when your hair is white with age. I made you and I will care for you. I will carry you along and be your Savior.   Isaiah 46:4 (TLB)

THE FIRST GENTLEMAN

*And Joseph arose from his sleep, and did as the angel of the Lord
commanded him, and took her as his wife, and kept her a virgin until
she gave birth to a Son; and he called His name Jesus.*
Matthew 1:24-25 (NAS)

*And he arose and took the Child and His mother by night, and
departed for Egypt. . . . And he arose and took the Child and His
mother and came into the land of Israel.* Matthew 2:14, 21 (NAS)

At Christmastime we do a lot of thinking and talking about
the Baby and the mother, as we should, for the Baby was the
first earthly glimpse man had ever had of his Creator.

Mary deserves our respect as the one God trusted enough to
let her care for such a One as he! But Joseph always gets the
short end of the stick in all the Christmas stories. He played
his part so well that he is taken for granted.

He accepted an embarrassing situation for his betrothed was
pregnant. He accepted it with good grace and had the faith to
believe that this truly was of God. He immediately assumed
the role of protector and gave up his rights as a husband. He
treated Mary with respect and gentleness in an age when men
treated women as one of their possessions. He set a whole new
pattern and standard for men to follow. He may have been the
very first gentleman as we know the term.

So, Joseph, thank you for living your life so nearly perfect
that we forget you. Thank you for the perfect example of what
a Christian gentleman can be.

Love each other with brotherly affection and take delight in honoring each other. Never be lazy in your work but serve the Lord enthusiastically.   Romans 12:10-11 (TLB)

There were about twenty young families, all filled with the spirit of adventure, living on that high Colorado plateau, altitude over 9,000 feet. They were all friends and were helping one another survive with little more than high hopes and hard work. They had all taken advantage of the Homestead Act. The men had built the homes, most of them log cabins. My dad carried the mail, my aunt and uncle ran the little grocery, and a friend taught school in a one-room schoolhouse. Entertainment was playing horseshoe and card games, having square dances and ice cream socials, the ice cream being made with blocks of ice cut from some high mountain lake. In the summer the men went out and rounded up wild ponies and we had our own rodeos.

I remember looking out the window of the log cabin at night to see coyotes silhouetted against the moonlit sky and hear their lonely howls.

Nothing much grew out there, except grain for feeding cattle. Winters were long and hard. The thing that made it bearable, even fun, was the spirit of adventure, the spirit of the frontier in all the people. Everybody helped everybody. They all helped raise one another's children. No amount of work was too much, if it meant a good joke or a surprise on somebody.

For a long time we did not even have a radio. I remember when the first one came in the mail. The nights were long and cold with only kerosene lamps for light and a potbellied stove for heat, and there was no entertainment. My mother used to be a schoolteacher, so it came natural to her to read to us in the long evenings. With my brother a young cowboy, and Dad a true frontiersman, you can bet she didn't read us *Little Women* or any other sissy tale. She read us Zane Grey's western novels. I probably heard them all, growing up. Dad had an old army blanket, made of rough wool and khaki colored. I'd pull it in behind the potbellied stove and wrap up in it and lie between the stove and the wall, as Mom read those tales to the three of us.

We never had Bible reading or prayer and I always regretted it, but now I see just how truly "devotional" that whole life-style really was.

It had nothing to do with the story. The security and love and warmth of the moment was doing the teaching. We were absorbing a sense of the magnitude of nature, the untamed glory of the mountains was becoming part of our spirits, and we were learning, through the hard life, a respect for people and for any living thing. Life was destructible, therefore precious. No one abused anyone else in that high valley.

Yes, it was devotional . . . not in words, but in meaning. I would happily wish just such an upbringing on any modern child—up to and including the "Zane Grey devotional hours."

THE TOTEM POLE

My little children, I am telling you this so that you will stay away from sin. But if you sin, there is someone to plead for you before the Father. His name is Jesus Christ, the one who is all that is good and who pleases God completely. He is the one who took God's wrath against our sins upon himself, and brought us into fellowship with God; and he is the forgiveness for our sins, and not only ours but all the world's. I John 2:1-2 (TLB)

One Sunday morning after church, our daughter Paula and I and the two grandchildren were trying to make it through lunch in one of Nashville's nice restaurants without too much ruckus. Both children were acting up, and the situation was getting tense and risky. Three-and-a-half-year-old Jamaica was pushing her luck and Paula was getting stern. A confrontation was in the making.

Jamaica got momentarily interested in part of the decor—a real totem pole. I prolonged my explanation of what a totem pole was, trying to keep the peace—all to no avail.

Finally Jamaica had enough ammunition. She whirled to her mother and said, "I don't like you! I'm going to carve you up into a totem pole!"

Her face registered triumph at her declaration—then changed to apprehension as she looked at me. "Is she your daughter?" she said. I nodded, "Yes." Eyes ablazing she said, "Do you *want* her?" I again answered, "Yes." To which she replied, "Well, then, *you* can have her!"

End of the matter—Paula was saved from the carver's knife!

By this time Paula and I were fighting tears, we were laughing so hard, and we beat a hasty farewell from the fine restaurant.

This same ritual goes on in the realm of the spirit all the time. The evil one, the prince of this world, is forever saying with triumph, "Aha! *Now* I'm going to carve you up and make you into the image of a false god." But if we are Christians, he knows he doesn't have final authority. He has to ask Jesus, who represents the Father, "Is she your daughter? Is he your son?" If the answer is yes, the next question will be, "Do you want her?" Because of who Jesus is, we know the answer will be yes. So there can be no other response than, "Well, *you* can have her."

And another battle with the enemy has been won.

Jesus is forever our advocate, the one who has the authority to see that we are eventually made into his image, not the image of a false god.

The One to whom we have given our hearts is forever claiming us as sons and daughters and fighting our battles for us.

"And if, as my representatives, you give even a cup of cold
water to a little child, you will surely be
rewarded."   Matthew 10:42 (TLB)

If you live in Minnesota or Wisconsin or Michigan and a big
snow is predicted to be on the way, you accept it. It's a way of
life and the snowplows fill up their gas tanks for all night
hauls. But if you live in the South, say Virginia or Tennessee,
and the news goes out that a "big snow is coming," everybody
runs to the grocery and gets ready to be stranded for a few
hours or days. The gentle South just isn't used to hard winter
ways.

On our country road in Tennessee, there were several little
houses of very poor people. I didn't know any of the people
who lived in those houses, but my twenty-year-old daughter
got to know some of them. She is a friendly little talker and
gets acquainted in grocery stores and filling stations.

The winter when the TV forecasters gleefully predicted that
the big snow was on its way, I rushed out to the store and got
groceries for the family, candles for emergencies, and logs for
the fireplace. I came back home feeling smug and self-satisfied.
My young daughter started home from work a little early, but
got to the house a bit late. "Why?" I inquired. "Well," she
said, "there's a little Mrs. Brown who lives in a shabby house
down by the gravel works place. Her mind is not very good
and she sort of wanders in and out of reality. I give her a ride

when she's walking to the store. I happened to go by. I was afraid she wouldn't be ready for a big snow, so I stopped to see her."

"What happened?" I said.

"I asked her if she knew a storm was coming and if she had enough food and would she like to go to the store. She wanted to know who would pay if she went, so I told her I would. We went and had a wonderful time, stocking up on a few things. It cost me thirty-eight dollars but it was worth it."

Since I am her mother, I know she only makes fifty dollars a week. It is enough to fill the gas tank in her car twice, or enough to fill up a hungry stomach for a little old lady, whose mind wanders a bit so that she can't remember to clean her house. But she is going to get caught by the big snow every bit as much as we who are much smugger and safer. By the way, I was much less smug and self-satisfied after Dee's arrival home.

No wonder Jesus' disciples were all young men. The young have tender hearts, thoughtful hearts, eager to give the cup of cold water.

"Make my heart young, Lord, and ever mindful of the big snows in other people's lives."

And each will be like a refuge from the wind,
And a shelter from the storm,
Like streams of water in a dry country,
Like the shade of a huge rock in a parched land.   *Isaiah 32:2 (NAS)*

We Americans are forever on a diet. We feel guilty over every extra calorie that makes its way inside. We have mistakenly made fat into our number one enemy and our number one sin. But there is good news in this morning's forecast! There is one place where we need to be fat! Hear me out now.

All good cooks know how to watch for the marbling in the beef—that's the little fat cells that make the meat tender when it's cooked. When you cook chicken, it's the fat on the skin that holds the juices in and makes wonderful moist and tender chicken. When you're baking pie crust, it's the fat that makes a flaky, tender crust. These delicious, mouth-watering foods we love to serve to family and friends.

To produce that extra fat, those cows and chickens had to be fed extra food—more food than they needed—to be good for us to eat. All that extra shortening in pie dough is more than you need to hold it together, but that is what makes the best pie crust.

There is a parallel here. If we get just enough food from our heavenly Father, through prayer, to barely get through the day, we will be like a person on a diet—lean and thin. If we pray enough and spend enough time with him, and get more spiritual food than we need to survive, we suddenly become spiritually fat and tender (just like a good steak). We become sensitive to other people and have something to share with them from our abundance. We can become food and sustenance, shelter and drink to them.

We become

> Like a refuge from the wind,
> And a shelter from the storm,
> Like streams of water in a dry country,
> Like the shade of a huge rock in a parched land.

We share our extra "fat" with them and they are nourished with spiritual food.

When it comes to prayer, we don't have to diet!

Say there! Is anyone thirsty? Come and drink—even if you have no money! Come, take your choice of wine and milk—it's all free! Why spend your money on foodstuffs that don't give you strength? Why pay for groceries that don't do you any good? Listen and I'll tell you where to get good food that fattens up your soul!
Isaiah 55:1-2 (TLB)

While he was eating, a woman came in with a bottle of very expensive perfume, and poured it over his head.

The disciples were indignant. "What a waste of good money," they said. "Why, she could have sold it for a fortune and given it to the poor."

Jesus knew what they were thinking and said, "Why are you criticizing her? For she has done a good thing to me. You will always have the poor among you, but you won't always have me. She has poured this perfume on me to prepare my body for burial. And she will always be remembered for this deed. The story of what she has done will be told throughout the whole world, wherever the Good News is preached."   Matthew 26:7-13 (TLB)

Most of us are perfume dabbers and sniffers. Who can resist the tester bottle on the department store counter? Two basic questions must be asked about every perfume. Does it smell good on me? And does the fragrance last? Our daughter DeeDee rolls down all the windows and gasps for air all the way home after we've been shopping together, because I try them all. A good day of shopping and perfume testing can force the family into the next room when we get home. But soon even the most expensive perfume fades and is gone.

There is, however, a type of fragrance that does not fade—the most desirable kind. It is the fragrance of Mary—the fragrance that wafts down to us through twenty centuries. Her love for Jesus was so pure, so all-consuming that she poured out upon him perfumed ointment that was worth about a year's wages. Her act of love makes our love stories seem paltry by comparison. She was seeking nothing, she was showing her love.

If, in the living, our lives can have something of Mary's fragrance about them, they surely will please him whom we love.

Mary's fragrance also answers the two basic questions about perfume. It will smell good on everybody and it will last.

SAMSON

*Be careful—watch out for attacks from Satan, your great
enemy. He prowls around like a hungry, roaring lion,
looking for some victim to tear apart.*   I Peter 5:8 (TLB)

We have some friends who bought a baby male African lion.
They named him Samson. At first they kept him in the house
like a puppy or kitten. He was easy to train and they enjoyed
him to the limit. Finally at about four and a half months, his
playing was getting too rough so they moved him outside to a
nice big fenced-in area and built him a house.

We were out there watching him play the other day. He has
his security blanket, like all kids, only he tries to carry his up
the tree, like his prey. Our friends also have goats, cows, and
ducks. Samson stalks them. They don't pay much attention to
him. Only the bull sees him as a threat. He turns and stares at
Samson with a challenge in his eye. When this happens,
Samson will cut and run for his master, Joel. It is funny to
watch. It also made me think. Sin is like that lion. At first the
sin is completely under our command. It will cut and run back
to us when there is danger.

But there's no way to stop it from growing in the normal
course of events, and pretty soon we are no longer the master.
Sin is the master and we're face to face with something that
can kill us. For our adversary, the devil, does indeed prowl
around like a lion, seeking someone to devour.

"And so, dear Father, advise us of the little Samsons in our
lives. Keep our hearts clean and under *your* command."

For I decided that I would speak only of Jesus Christ and his death on the cross. I came to you in weakness—timid and trembling. And my preaching was very plain, not with a lot of oratory and human wisdom, but the Holy Spirit's power was in my words, proving to those who heard them that the message was from God. I did this because I wanted your faith to stand firmly upon God, not on man's great ideas. I Corinthians 2:2-5 (TLB)

There are more tales to tell about Samson, the pet lion. He finally got big enough that his playing was a little more than could be handled without a first-aid kit nearby. So his owners took him to the vet and had him declawed. Some things you just have to deal with! After he loses his baby teeth and gets his mature teeth, he is in for another shock. His teeth are going to be ground down and capped, so they can't do the usual amount of damage.

We were watching him play again one day. He has a special tree in the yard that he likes to sharpen his claws on. He also likes to practice climbing up the tree with his imagined prey, the security blanket. This day after his paws were healed from the declawing process he ran to the tree and attacked it with his usual force. The paws, instead of catching, just slid down the tree to the ground. Samson looked astounded! What was wrong? He tried it again and again. It is his nature to—but to no avail.

It is the nature of most people to keep trying, giving it "the old college try," but unless they're committed to the Lord's control, their lives have no grip, no claws, no bite. They go through futile motions, making no mark, climbing no trees.

Even Samson's name reminds me that it is possible to lose the power of God out of our lives. For while the Old Testament Samson slept, just like Samson the lion, his power was taken from him.

Paul speaks to this matter of knowing where the power is, in today's scripture verses: that your faith should not rest on the wisdom of men, but on the power of God.

But Jesus gave her no reply—not even a word. . . .
"Woman," Jesus told her, "your faith is large, and your
request is granted." And her daughter was healed right
then.   Matthew 15:23a, 28 (TLB)

When people approached Jesus without love, he was silent. The Canaanite woman had heard of him and his healings. She apparently had heard of him like she had heard of witch doctors who might help her. When she begged him to cast the devil from her daughter, Jesus answered her not a word. As she continued to ask, he finally said, "It is not meet to take the children's bread, and to cast it to dogs."

The difference between children and dogs or people and animals is the ability to know and to love. She had been so intent in her scrutiny of him that something quickened in her heart, some belief, some love, and she said, "Truth, Lord: yet the dogs eat of the crumbs which fall from their master's table."

By that statement she made him the loving Master and herself the hungry, unloving dog—a correct assessment of the facts. He was moved by her grasp of the issue, and said, "O woman, great is thy faith: be it unto thee even as thou wilt."

And the child was made whole. It was a miracle of love.

"Mary!" Jesus said. She turned toward him.
  "Master!" she exclaimed.   John 20:16 (TLB)

"What do you want me to do for you?" Jesus asked.
  "Oh, teacher," the blind man said, "I want to see!"
                                            Mark 10:51 (TLB)

Marijohn Wilkin has a lovely song "How Old Were You?"

There they were, ordinary people doing their ordinary tasks, teaching the little children the laws of God. Then one day there was a Child who brought them up short. Now they were dealing with something outside their experience, something they couldn't name or define. It arrested their hearts so they hesitated to speak of it to one another. This Child already knew! It left them befuddled, awed; they didn't know how to handle it.

Karen, our daughter, is a first-grade teacher. One of her new little girls can read. She asked the child's kindergarten teachers, "Did you teach her to read?" "No," was the reply. "She didn't read last year."

Karen called her mother. "Did you teach your little girl to read over summer vacation?"

"No," she said. "She reads her books to me, but I thought she had memorized them by listening. I didn't know she could read!"

Karen and the other teachers stirred it around among themselves, but there was no answer except that the child could read and no one had taught her!

We can just imagine how those other teachers felt.

"How is it that this carpenter's Child already knows the things we are to teach him?"

Oh, great wise men of old, if you had known, you would have frightened all the other children by throwing yourselves at his childish feet!

For this is he who was with the Father and who created all that is—

This is he, who is to bear your burden to a cross.

This is he, who has power and dominion over all things!

This is he, whom the blind man soon will call, "Rabboni," which is to say, "Master, Teacher!"

It serves you well, teachers, to be in awe of this Child!

"But when you give alms, do not let your left hand know what your right hand is doing."   Matthew 6:3 (NAS)

But thou, when thou prayest, enter into thy closet, and when thou hast shut thy door, pray to thy Father which is in secret; and thy Father which seeth in secret shall reward thee openly.
Matthew 6:6 (NAVES)

Why does the Lord ask us for secrecy in the act of giving to others and in the area of communication with him? It seems to me, the reason has to do with love.

Hear this tale. We knew we were in trouble when we saw the ring. Two of the girls and Doug and I were at the Nashville Flea Market at a jewelry dealer's booth. There it was, the most outlandish man's ring we had ever seen. It was big! I'm talking monstrous. We knew Doug would love it. And he did!

Doug hardly ever wants anything for himself, but we knew he wanted *that* ring. It was way too much money, though, and we all went away feeling cast down. Doug left town for a concert on Saturday. But since the Flea Market was still in town, the girls and I went back on Sunday. We had to look at the ring again. As we came down the aisle, the jewelry lady waved at us and said excitedly, "I've been trying to call you. Aren't you Doug Oldham's family?" We gave an affirmative nod. "My husband and I are Christians and we recognized you. We talked last night about how much Doug liked that ring. Would you like to put it on the installment plan for Christmas, with a considerable discount figured in?"

Would we! That gave us six months to pay it off. We made a lot of secret trips to the Flea Market over the next months, and a lot of payments, but we made it. By Christmas the ring was ours. We were so excited we could hardly stand it. This year Daddy Doug was getting a real gift. And it was still a secret! When Christmas finally came and Doug got the ring, he cried and we cried and everybody present cried and it was wonderful. Why? Because he knew that we loved him enough to do some real wheeling and dealing to get him a gift. And we knew that he knew. It was great!

In the process, we had to keep our left hand from knowing what our right hand was doing in order to give him a special gift. Love was the reason. (When Doug and I shut the door to go to sleep on that Christmas night, I told him how I loved him in words known *only* to him. Love was the reason.)

Just so does the heavenly Father want us to shut the door to others and enter into a secret place and talk to him in words of love spoken only to him.

In the same way when we give a good gift to someone here on earth and do it in his name and for his sake, it should not be for show, for others to see, but for him alone, who is our beloved.

He is not asking for something strange or irrational in these two requests. He is asking for our love.

And now just as you trusted Christ to save you, trust him, too, for each day's problems; live in vital union with him. Let your roots grow down into him and draw up nourishment from him. See that you go on growing in the Lord, and become strong and vigorous in the truth you were taught. Let your lives overflow with joy and thanksgiving for all he has done. Colossians 2:6-7 (TLB)

Strange creatures that we are, we all love a big show. Once while watching one of these big shows, I saw a very unusual finale. I was sitting in our bus in front of a church, watching the comings and goings of an afternoon wedding. The people were strangers, but it was wonderful, nevertheless. There was a flurry between church and reception hall. There were girls in long flowing blue gowns and fellows in black tuxedos, and lots of other people. Some of these folks looked pleased, some looked worried. The bride and groom in royal wedding regalia crossed from the hall into the church. They changed into going-away clothes and came back to the entrance of the hall where family and friends were gathered for a final farewell. Then came the rice throwing, picture taking, and hugging and kissing. Finally, the couple got into an outlandishly decorated car and drove off. It was a big to-do.

The people began to disperse. Obviously, all of them were the people who were the very closest and dearest to this couple. After a few minutes here came the car again, tin cans and balloons careening behind, and two beaming faces within.

They couldn't resist. They had come back for a final, triumphal swoop past the church.

It was a big disappointment. The folks who were leaving, going to their cars or back into the church, barely noted their passing. They looked and nodded or half-raised a hand. It was as much as to say, "We gave you a good launching, now you're on your own. Do your own sailing."

That final scene struck my heart. People can do a lot of supporting and launching us, but they can't do the real living for us. That couple is now strictly on their own. They have to make it work. They will have to talk to each other enough and love each other enough to continually know each other.

It's the same way with being a Christian. Other people can support us, launch us, give us the Big Hoorah, but we have to do the living. It's just me and the Lord, building my inner spirit and soul. That's something nobody else can do. I have to talk to him enough and love him enough, to continually know him. If I made a final swoop past the church where I came to know him, probably nobody would notice. We're on our own.

Don't worry about anything; instead, pray about everything;
tell God your needs and don't forget to thank him for his
answers. Philippians 4:6 (TLB)

One lovely summer evening our house guest reached for the red phone in the living room and dialed a long distance number. When her four-year-old granddaughter was on the line she said, "Tracie, darling, what would you like for your birthday?" The answer came back quick as an echo, "I'd love to have a dolly—and one for Ashley."

We laughed about how the little rascal had conned her grandmother into getting something for her little sister, too.

The next day we went shopping and Marie bought two dolls. Is there a grandmother anywhere who would have purchased one? They were sister dolls—one a little bigger than the other—both in calico dresses, all packaged together.

"And one for Ashley" is the most basic impulse and expression of love in the world. Upon this same impulse have the great charities been started, schools built, hospitals set up and paid for, and missionaries sent to dark lands. The preachers and evangelists that have trod the earth have done so because something in their hearts said, "Ashley must also have this wonderful gift that I have received." And since they know the Lord's heart as a four-year-old knows her grandmother's heart, they have the courage to ask of him in advance, "Please send one for Ashley." And because his heart is more true than any grandmother's heart, he has promised to answer our requests.

Then they continued northward toward Bethel where he had camped before, between Bethel and Ai—to the place where he had built the altar. And there he again worshiped the Lord. Genesis 13:3-4 (TLB)

One year we made a move farther north than where we had been living. We decided to move in March, packed in April, moved the first of May, started to settle in all of that month and on into June. In the South, in our old home, March and April were already warm. In our new home, in the North, May and early June were still cool. I kept thinking, "Spring is lasting so long this year." Then I remembered it was because we had moved to a harder, more severe climate.

In order to experience the springtime of spiritual life—the time of the first love, the way we felt and thought when we were first converted, we need to keep moving. We must have the nerve to move to a colder climate, a harder territory, to experience the springtime. The Lord draws near to us and gives us his sweetness when we're trusting him completely.

We probably get hot and tired and listless as Christians, because we stay too far south where life is easy. If we spiritually move north where life is harder, we can experience a longer springtime of the spirit.

When Abraham said, "Give me hill country," God came to him and renewed his promise to him, saying that he would give him the land forever. Abraham found his springtime.

Lot stayed in the valley.

If you shout a pleasant greeting to a friend too early in the morning, he will count it as a curse!   Proverbs 27:14 (TLB)

Proverbs 27:14 is one of Doug's favorite verses. Don't give him any shocks in the morning. Don't jolt the precarious balance of the senses in any way. Tread very softly until after he's had his bacon, eggs, juice, and coffee.

Family life may very well rise and fall on how we treat one another in the morning. A little graciousness, a little carefulness, a little companionable elbow room will do a lot to set the day off right.

The Jewish family at the time of Christ had spoken benedictions for all the routines of the day. There were eighteen in all. The morning benediction was spoken aloud before anything else was said.

First, there was the waking greeting which was exchanged instead of "good morning." It was "Blessed be he who loveth his people Israel." This was followed by the morning benediction which was, "O my God, the soul which thou gavest me is pure; thou didst create it, thou didst form it, thou didst breathe it into me. Thou preservest it within me, and thou wilt take it from me, but wilt restore unto me hereafter. So long as the soul is within me, I will give thanks unto thee, O Lord my God and God of my fathers, Sovereign of all works, Lord of all souls! Blessed art thou, O Lord, who restorest souls unto the dead."

It is an unusual way to start the day, and strange to our modern mind, but nevertheless a wonderful way. No loud shouts that will be counted a curse.

It is even possible to simplify it and say with a whole heart today, "Let everything that hath breath praise the Lord. Praise ye the Lord" (Ps. 150:6).

Know ye not that ye are the temple of God, and that the Spirit of God dwelleth in you?   I Corinthians 3:16

What? know ye not that your body is the temple of the Holy Ghost which is in you, which ye have of God, and ye are not your own?   I Corinthians 6:19

A few years back my father-in-law made a trip to England. He is a minister and a history buff, so everything had great meaning and interest to him. On this particular day, he was touring London, and was in Westminster Abbey. The young guide was pointing out the various types of architecture and was telling about the many years involved in the building of the Abbey. He viewed the many tombs of famous people—poets, writers, kings. It was grand, and far from boring. But one particular little old lady in the group was of a very practical turn of mind. Dr. Dale heard her say to herself, as if to reassure herself, "This is a *church*, isn't it?"

She must have arrived at her own conclusion for pretty soon in a nice, clear, carrying voice, she said to the guide, "Young man! Young man! Anybody been *saved* here lately?"

There were lots of polite, strained smiles on the faces of the people in the group, but it struck my father-in-law's funny bone and he still laughs about it.

She is right, of course, the real purpose of any *building* that is a temple of worship, is to create *people* who are temples, temples with legs. These are the kinds of "places of worship" that can carry the gospel of peace to a troubled world. It is forever easy to get overly involved with the building of something and forget what it is for in the first place.

Little lady! Little lady! Keep asking your outlandish questions!

We the two-legged temples need the reminder.

I am Jehovah; there is no other God. I will strengthen you and send you out to victory even though you don't know me, and all the world from east to west will know there is no other God. I am Jehovah and there is no one else. I alone am God. I form the light and make the dark. I send good times and bad. I, Jehovah, am he who does these things.   Isaiah 45:5-7 (TLB)

"I believe God either causes *or* permits *everything*, and I cannot tell the difference." Pastor Billy Ball said those words as part of a Sunday morning sermon.

Those words and that premise can ring like a silver bell and be the clear and ringing chime of freedom for any man—even for any Christian. You say, "Oh, Christians already believe that." Well, I for one have been guilty of not believing it at all times. It is an idea that we handle like a dog does his rawhide chew. We chew it and worry it to a pulp, but we cannot, or do not, eat it and digest it—and believe it.

Here is a parallel. The slaves were freed in English-held lands, thirty years before slaves were freed in America. In Jamaica when this happened, a group of the slaves held a ceremony. They placed an open coffin in a hollowed-out grave in the ground. They gathered around and sang and spoke of their new freedom. They each carried something in their hands. They held some symbol of their slavery—a whip with a thong on the end—a ball and chain—pieces of rope—pickaxes that had made their days a misery. They began to chant and march around the open casket. Each man in turn threw into that casket his symbol of slavery and as it fell gave a shout of freedom. He was free! Then they closed the lid and shoveled on the dirt! Slavery was gone!

So can we march around that open casket of doubt about God and his true power. Did he *cause* the things that have happened in my life? Or did he permit them?

Being finite I cannot tell the difference. But if it came under his authority either way, then I can throw my persisting doubt or anxiety into the casket and cover it over with the good fresh dirt of his care and keeping. Those doubts and fears that chain me and make life a drudgery are gone! And he is Lord!

Ring the bell of freedom!

THE HIGHEST PLACE

His home is in Jerusalem. He lives upon Mount
Zion.   Psalm 76:2 (TLB)

The tour bus driver made the necessary adjustments in gears
and speed as we traveled up the road with the haunting name,
"from Jerusalem to Jericho." It is a road surely traveled by all
those people whose names are so familiar to us. The old
prophets, like Jeremiah, came this way, as did a band of
rag-tag boys who were disciples of the young man called Jesus.
The Inn of the Good Samaritan is on this road. It is a wild and
barren and desolate area. The ground, the soil, the rocks all
look *so old*.

The ground is gray with age, gray with the dust of many
bones. The sharp-edged beauty of the rocks has been worn
away by time, time, time, and the rocks are like rounded,
stooped shoulders bowed with age and care.

Something strange was happening to my heart as we drove
into that ancient city. In spite of all the ordinary commotion of
a tour bus, there was an ethereal look and feel to the city.
There was a confirmation in my heart, in tune with all time
that proclaimed this city to be "the Highest Place on Earth." I
felt I was standing on a higher place than even when we stood
on the top of Mt. Evans in the Rockies.

The houses are made of the old stone of the earth and they
take on a pale unearthly glow, so that houses and land blend
into each other. And the light! What is it about the light in that

city? It lies low to the earth and seems to come from *under* those gnarled old olive trees, instead of from the sky above. Sometimes it is a clear, white penetrating light. Sometimes it is a golden glow that permeates everything.

There is no denying it. Jerusalem is a city set on a hill, set apart, beloved of God, lived in by earthly Jesus. His presence is there. And because it is there, Jerusalem is and forever shall be the highest place on earth!

PILLOW OF PEACE

I will both lay me down in peace, and sleep: for thou, Lord, only makest me dwell in safety.   Psalm 4:8 (NAVES)

When thou liest down, thou shalt not be afraid: yea, thou shalt lie down, and thy sleep shall be sweet.   Proverbs 3:24 (NAVES)

He shall enter into peace: they shall rest in their beds, each one walking in his uprightness.   Isaiah 57:2 (NAVES)

"When I lay my head down at night, I put it on a pillow of peace." A young college student spoke those words in his testimony about how wonderful it was to be a new Christian.

That experience is one of the true luxuries of life. It is one of the hidden treasures that we can keep on seeking and finding. Long after I was a Christian, I still had some terrible, numbing fears. I can pinpoint the spiritual skirmishes that were won with those fears and likewise can pinpoint the final victory. The final battle was won when I saw that the central issue was whether I thought God could defeat the devil and his evil power in the world, when it came to my own personal safety. It was humiliating to realize that, even as a Christian, by my fear I was saying that I actually thought the devil was more powerful than God. When I asked him to forgive me for that disbelief and told him I would trust him to protect me from personal harm, the battle with fear was won.

I am often alone, for Doug is a traveling man, but when I lay my head down at night, I put it on a pillow of peace.

Therefore, since we have so great a cloud of witnesses surrounding us,
let us also lay aside every encumbrance, and the sin which so easily
entangles us, and let us run with endurance the race that is set before
us. Hebrews 12:1 (NAS)

To be a grandparent is to have a view from a high hill. You
remember starting in the valley with your small babies and
struggling and working your way up that hill. There were so
many obstacles in the way—the trees, the rocks, the streams to
be forded. You carry your children's weight as well as your
own, and you're walking uphill. There are wolves along the
way, so you stay close together. You build your own fire for
warmth and huddle close together. You have very little panorama, very little overview, and it's very hard to make it
through each day.

But to be a grandparent is to have reached the top of that
hill, to be able to look down and see the panorama, see the
overview of what is happening in the valley and the long, hard
climb. You can look at the new family working its way up the
hill and have great compassion, because you know what it's
like—you've made the climb. There is much made of grandparents loving too much—of spoiling their grandchildren. It's
only because they see it all so much more clearly than they did
when they were the climbers.

This is a wonderful parallel to those who have gone on
before us to the high hill of heaven. The Bible tells us that as
Christians we have a "cloud of witnesses" about us—watching.

These Christians that have gone on before may be watching our slow and painful, dangerous progress up the high hill of life. They are compassionate because they've made the climb. They now have the panorama, they understand, they have the overview.

Someday we also will be part of this cloud of witnesses and then we will know—the best view of all is the view from the high hill of heaven!

And the work of righteousness shall be peace; and the effect of righteousness quietness and assurance for ever. And my people shall dwell in a peaceable habitation, and in sure dwellings, and in quiet resting places. Isaiah 32:17-18 (NAVES)

When she was little we used to call Paula "the Blackeyed Pea" because of her expressive black eyes. She was a very little girl when she gave me her pointed opinion about some drop-in guests who had just left our home.

"They broke the air," she observed, black eyes snapping in exasperation. She was right. There was a certain peaceful home atmosphere that had been shattered, like a rock hitting a windowpane, when they arrived. It made me wonder about their true motives.

When the Lord has command of the inner life, there is a sense of the person's spirit and personality having rounded corners, not jagged edges that can "break the air" around other people. Today I'm praying for rounded corners for my spirit.

Thou wilt keep him in perfect peace, whose mind is stayed on thee. Isaiah 26:3*a* (NAVES)

"Again, the Kingdom of Heaven is like a pearl merchant on the lookout for choice pearls. He discovered a real bargain—a pearl of great value—and sold everything he owned to purchase it!" Matthew 13:45-46 (TLB)

I've thought a lot about Tom since I started this book. It is very unlikely that he would ever read it, so it's safe to tell you a little about him. Tom was one of Paula's friends in college. He was brilliant, clever, creative, a quick wit, and a rebel of vascillating proportions—meaning sometimes he was a rebel, sometimes he wasn't. Paula thought he was great. He came from a wonderful Christian family, but somehow the whole Christian concept eluded him.

His family lived across the country, so they wrote him often. In her warm and regular letters, his mother often included a copy of *Our Daily Bread,* a well-known devotional. Now Tom loved his mother but he *hated,* I mean really hated *Our Daily Bread.* He would rip it out of the envelope and throw it vehemently across the mail room, before settling down to read the letter. Paula loved this little ritualistic drama and also thought it exceedingly funny. Something too good to pass by. One day she retrieved one of these whirled copies after he left the mail room and carefully printed on the cover, "Property of Tom _____." She then put it on the coffee table in the student lounge. You can be sure he found out—and was he mad! He probably never forgave her. She didn't care, she still thought it was wonderful!

They also had some very serious conversations about Jesus and the personal Christian life. Somehow it baffled him. But in their conversations he said, "I'll tell you, Paula, if I ever meet this Jesus, as you describe him, you'll be the first to know. I'll phone from wherever I am."

Tom is now a medical doctor, all properly graduated and working . . . somewhere. There is not a chance in this world that he'd ever read *this* book, but, just in case miracles do happen—"Dear Tom, Paula's still waiting for your call.

Love,

Paula's mother."

THE AUCTION

Thou art my portion, O Lord: I have said that I would keep thy
words. . . . I am thine, save me; for I have sought thy precepts. . . .
I have sworn, and I will perform it, that I will keep thy righteous
judgments.   Psalm 119:57, 94, 106 (NAVES)

One man waggled his finger about an inch and the auctioneer raised the bid by three thousand dollars. Then his eyes
went to our friend who was bidding for us, all the while
chanting rather quietly his auctioneer's song. Our agent nodded his head the least bit, and up went the bid. Our hearts
were beating fast, but there were no voices to be heard, and no
noise from the little group of people gathered just inside the
courthouse door. After making the rounds of the people more
than a few times to be sure he had the highest bid, he pointed
to our agent friend and said, "Sold!" We couldn't believe it!
We had just bought a house! With that almost imperceptible
nod of the head, the single biggest investment of our lives had
been made. We had to back it up with a certain amount of cold
cash yet that day, and the financing for the rest in thirty days.

I turned to John, our son-in-law, and said, "This gives me
goose bumps. It feels like getting married or something." He
said, "Yeah! Like getting married at the gambling tables in Las
Vegas!" Granted! The whole thing was a gamble.

I couldn't help being amazed at how silently that enormous
transaction was made. There were no trumpets, no drum rolls,
no special speakers. The silent nod of the head carried the
intent of the heart and mind to follow through with the

money, the hard work, the change in direction for the whole life. It is also true of virtually all our basic lifetime decisions. They're made in the heart and the mind and made solid in silence, then the least nod of the head, the opening of the arms, the quiet, choked, "I do," or whispered, "Yes, I will" carry us in one basic fateful step to another level of life.

Our decisions in favor of or against our Friend Jesus are made the same way. Very silently, very solidly our smallest cry or prayer or decision is heard and answered and recorded by the Lord.

No wonder Phillips Brooks wrote those glorious words that say, "How silently, how silently the wondrous gift is given!" in his hymn "O Little Town of Bethlehem." The gift of the Son is given silently to our hearts today.

I trained him from infancy, I taught him to walk, I held him in my arms. But he doesn't know or even care that it was I who raised him.
As a man would lead his favorite ox, so I led Israel with my ropes of love. I loosened his muzzle so he could eat. I myself have stooped and fed him. Hosea 11:3-4 (TLB)

But when you had eaten and were satisfied, then you became proud and forgot me. Hosea 13:6 (TLB)

These are heartbreaking verses. They show us how God feels. When we come to him to start our life with him, he teaches us to walk, carries us in his arms of protection, heals us when we don't recognize where the healing comes from, lifts the bit from our mouths and bends down to feed us. But, as we eat, we become satisfied with ourselves, with life; and being satisfied we become proud. We begin to say, "I did it. With my own innate ability, I have overcome, I have succeeded." And then . . . we forget him.

This natural, earthly pull away from God happens with people, with institutions, with churches, with countries. The prince of this world, Satan, makes the pull away from God seem right to man.

It reminds me of my granddaughter at three and a half years. Since her birth her mother had lovingly fed her with her hand, healed her hurts, taught her to talk, taught her to walk. But now that she could do all these things, she was proud—proud of herself and her accomplishments. So one day when she was mad at her mother she said with fire in her eye, "You can't be my mommy anymore."

Pride was the culprit, just as pride is the culprit when we, in effect say, "You can't be my Lord anymore." It doesn't change the facts. Paula is still Jamaica's mother just as God is still our Father. All that has been added is the hurt.

Finally, brethren, whatsoever things are true, whatsoever things are
honest, whatsoever things are just, whatsoever things are pure,
whatsoever things are lovely, whatsoever things are of good report; if
there be any virtue, and if there be any praise, think on these
things. Philippians 4:8

We used to live down a two-lane, bumpy country road. In a
five-mile stretch of that road, there is a marvelous selection of
scenes you won't find on a super highway. There are pigs,
goats, mules, horses, cows, tobacco fields, hay fields, lovely
hills, a one-room country store called Duke's Green Acres, and
a Confederate Medical Clinic. (I don't know what you do if you
cut your finger and you're a Yankee.) There is a little cafe that
advertises "Chitlin' Dinners on Friday nights." In the years we
drove down that road, all these things were a constant source
of interest to me.

However, one thing on that road is so ugly that it's not only
uninteresting, but it's almost a crime. It is a car cemetery,
where car carcasses are piled in big heaps, with no one having
the decency to bury them. The wrecks crowd out onto the road
in a most dangerous manner, making me wonder if the owner
happens to be a brother of the county road commissioner!

I was always so involved in getting around this mess that I
never looked at the farm across the road. One evening, as
Doug and I drove by that place on the road, a big beautiful
peacock went strolling across the road in front of us, trailing
his long brilliant tail feathers behind him. We were so

astounded we stopped the car in the middle of the road and let him cross! I mean, what else can you do? He was beautiful!

The next time I drove that road, I forgot to be mad at the junk cars on the one side of the road because I was looking in the farmyard on the other side of the road for the peacocks. Sure enough, there they were, several gorgeous peacocks! They live there! After that, I saw them every day! They had been there the whole year I'd been driving that road. I was too incensed by the ugliness on the one side of the road to see the regal, exotic beauty on the other side.

The Bible tells us about the two sides of the road. It even tells us on which side to look!

Finally, brethren, . . . whatsoever things are lovely, . . . think on these things.

THE VOICE OF LOVE

My sheep recognize my voice, and I know them, and they
follow me.   John 10:27 (TLB)

Once on a cold winter's night, I was awakened from a sound
sleep by the voice of my husband calling out sharply, "Laura!"
It was a warning tone of voice that he would use if I suddenly
stepped in front of a moving car. He was not in the room or
even in the house, but many miles away on tour. I was
instantly awake and sat up to see what was wrong. Moving
around cautiously to check things out, I saw footprints in the
snow where someone had been standing outside my bedroom
window. A voice of love had called out to warn me of danger.

I believe that it was angelic protection, but the angel had
chosen to use the one voice I would respond to instantly—the
voice of love. A stranger's voice would have been confusing
and the meaning misunderstood—but not that voice.

In the tenth chapter of John, we who belong to the Lord are
spoken of as his sheep. The fourteenth verse says, "I am the
good shepherd, and know my sheep, and am known of mine,"
and the sixteenth verse says, "And they shall hear my voice."

He wants us to know him so well that we will instantly
know his voice. He desires that his voice be so familiar to us,
we can easily discern its meaning. It may be easier than we
realize, for it is always easy to understand the voice of love.

For I will pour water upon him that is thirsty, and floods upon the dry ground: I will pour my spirit upon thy seed, and my blessing upon thine offspring:
   And they shall spring up as among the grass, as willows by the water courses.   Isaiah 44:3-4

John is our son-in-law and travels with Doug to help in the concerts. He is a keen observer and is interested in everything and everybody. One day he told us what he sees as he watches different people perform before Christian audiences.

He sees the audience as kind, wonderful people, most of them tired, all of them thirsty. They have come for a drink of spiritual water. If it's an evening where there are several performers, the audience will be treated to a variety of experiences.

But, says John, over the years, as he has watched, performers have begun to fall in two basic groups. There are the empty decorated steins and there are the crystal cups full of water. He says the people are usually kind, saying in effect, "What a beautiful stein we saw tonight." But since, whether they knew it or not, they came for a drink, the only true measure of success is whether they saw a crystal cup and through it to the water and then received a drink.

I never heard a better description of a worldly man doing his best and a spiritual man letting the Spirit work through him.

As the crystal cup pours out water upon people, "They shall spring up . . . as willows by the water courses."

At that point, the concert is a success.

And a large crowd soon gathered where Jesus was; but
as they saw the man sitting there, fully clothed and
perfectly sane, they were frightened.   Mark 5:15 (TLB)

Doug looked up one night during the intermission of one of
his concerts to see an arresting looking young girl making her
way across the stage toward him. She had on precariously high
heels, skin-tight straight-legged jeans, no bra, and a very skimpy
top that let you know about the bra.

"I won't be here for the second half," she said. "I'm going
home."

When she received no reply, she continued. "I really got
condemned in this program tonight and I've just given my heart
to the Lord. I'm going home to put some clothes on!" And away
she went. I didn't ask, but I doubt if she got a reply from my
husband, even then. I mean, some things just leave a man
speechless!

This cute little girl has a pretty good chance of making it in
the Christian life. Her instincts are good. She might not know
the stories in the Bible that gave precedence to her action, but
there are some.

There was the demoniac who lived naked among the tombs.
After he met Jesus and was cleansed of the demons, people saw
him *clothed* and in his right mind, sitting at the feet of Jesus.

I wish you well, young girl. You're living in a society that
doesn't encourage either being clothed or in your right mind,

and certainly not sitting at the feet of Jesus. You've just made a step that will put you *out* of step with this world, but *in* step with the marching feet of saints and angels, martyrs, and heavenly hosts starting out on a walk that never ends—through the wonders of this world, and right on into the mysterious reaches of heaven.

You can afford to miss the second half of the concert. Your life is going to be full!

And Jesus said, Let her alone; why trouble ye her? she hath wrought a good work on me.   Mark 14:6

Jesus was very gracious to women. Perhaps he was the first man ever to understand them and goodness knows they are an enigma upon the earth! He broke all the rules of the day and talked with the woman at the well. She certainly wasn't a virtuous woman, but neither was she hateful and vindictive. She responded with love and belief and a willingness to tell who she was, in order to tell who he was! In other words, she was a true witness.

He also loved Mary, who was a dreamer, a thinker, a romantic, and thoroughly impractical. He responded to her dreams and her thoughts and her love for him.

He loved Martha, too, however. He chastised her gently for her work-worn spirit, but he clearly loved her. He wanted her to balance things out, to be able to know what was best in life. He loved her for the way she created a warm home and cared for others.

He loved the woman who was called a sinner who poured the alabaster box of ointment on his feet and washed them with her tears. He saw a broken heart and a contrite loving spirit and he made a spectacle of himself in order to heal her heart.

He faced a mob of angry men armed with stones ready to

kill a woman accused of adultery, sent the men slinking away, and restored the woman to life with dignity.

Though both men and women should love our Lord Jesus for what he has done for them, sometimes I think women should love him the most. He gave them their "personhood." At his coming, they became something of value. If he loved so greatly these very imperfect women whose stories are recorded in the Bible, surely he loves women today and does what no earthly man can ever do. He *understands* them!

I have placed my rainbow in the clouds as a sign of my promise until the end of time, to you and to all the earth. When I send clouds over the earth, the rainbow will be seen in the clouds, and I will remember my promise to you and to every being, that never again will the floods come and destroy all life.   Genesis 9:13-15 (TLB)

She was only three and a half and her Bible stories told her that there was such a thing as a rainbow. It was a beautiful, graceful bow of colors arching up in the sky after a rain. But she could not remember having seen one. Riding along in the car with her mother and grandmother on the right kind of day for rainbows, she kept searching the sky. Finally she cried with intense feeling, "But I *need* a rainbow."

Forthwith she began to *pray* for one, to the consternation of her mother and grandmother, neither of whom could produce one.

There was no rainbow that day but about three weeks later a perfect rainbow appeared in the sky. The little girl had an unobstructed view from her own backyard. Her joy was real and her heart was full. Her "need" had been met!

We, too, need rainbows. Rainbows follow storms. But if there is no sun, there never is a rainbow. The rainbow is spoken of as a covenant between God and man. It is God's promise that he will not utterly destroy mankind with water again. So, in our lives, if we have the *Son* in our heart, the Living Light, we have his promise that he will not destroy us.

But if we have not the Living Light, the Son, there can be destruction and judgment.

She was absolutely right, that little one. Jamaica did *need* a rainbow.

Her need is my need, the need of all mankind. We need the Son. We need his promise of love after the storm.

THE FIGHTING SISTERS

Now Jesus loved Martha, and her sister, and Lazarus.   John 11:5

We can't say we haven't been warned. The story of Martha and Mary explains perfectly that there are two types of women in the world, not only in the world outside, but also the world inside. Every woman has both a Mary and a Martha living inside her mind and emotions. And very often they are fighting—slugging it out and making her miserable.

There is the splendid Martha. She is the nest maker, the practical worker. She loves to cook and clean and organize, making things nice for others to enjoy. Nothing in this world would run right, if it were not for Martha. She is absolutely indispensable. Every lovely, orderly home in the world is because of Martha.

Then there is Mary. She is the one who brings the sunshine. She loves and thinks and laughs and dances and dreams. She is very impractical—but absolutely indispensable. Nobody would enjoy life if it were not for Mary.

We're blessed that every woman has both a Martha and a Mary in her make-up. The trick is to get them to quit fighting and to strike the proper balance. The world isn't helping much. It seems as though some of its propaganda is trying to turn us into Peter and John.

My prayer is that the Lord will guide every seeking female heart to the proper perspective, the proper balance between those two inward fighting sisters, Martha and Mary.

THE SHOPPING CART

[He] satisfieth thy mouth with good things; so that thy youth is renewed like the eagle's.   Psalm 103:5

For he satisfieth the longing soul, and filleth the hungry soul with goodness.   Psalm 107:9

Paula tried everything to keep fifteen-month-old Baby John quiet, but to no avail. He felt antisocial, and antisocial he would be, so she finally left the meeting where we were and went outside to pass the time and wait for us. We were near a shopping area, but she had no money. She was aggravated and bored. She wandered into one of those superduper-drug-hardware-department discount places and took a cart to put Baby John in and give her arms a rest. Then—the temptation was too much—and besides she felt at odds with the world.

She began to look seriously at the merchandise. As she wandered up and down the aisles she put into the cart the things she *really* wanted and would buy if she could. Some food items, some clothing, some drug items, some toys—all chosen leisurely and very carefully. The selection took a great deal of time and stirred up her interest and imagination enough that she conquered the aggravation and the blahs.

Finally, she realized the rest of us would soon be coming out of our meeting in the other building, and she had to leave. She wheeled right up near the check-out, picked up Baby John, left the loaded basket and walked out—feeling as free as air. When she told us how she had passed the time, we howled. I'm not recommending it as therapy, you understand. Somebody had to replace all that merchandise. But something about her action puts a tug on your heart. We are all *so* human, we need so many things, want so much, have real needs and longings and desires. And like a friend of ours used to say, "The Lord knows all about it." He has provisions for those needs. He knows exactly what we should put in our shopping cart to satisfy those needs, and furthermore he has the money to pay the bill, and make them ours.

He "made provision" for us long ago and knows how to fill the hungry soul with goodness!

THE NOVICE

On every Lord's Day each of you should put aside something from
what you have earned during the week, and use it for this offering.
The amount depends on how much the Lord has helped you earn.

I Corinthians 16:2 (TLB)

He was a turquoise jewelry dealer and moved from place to place, following the flea markets and antique shows around. For some reason known only to himself, he began to read the Bible. He was first astounded, then convicted, then saved! Now here he was with a whole new perception of life and he had to tell the tale. He told some friends of ours. They were thrilled because they knew what he was talking about because they were already Christians. But as he shared his findings, they were astounded!

He had read in that Bible that he was to share, to tithe, as it were. Since he had no background in church formats and hadn't heard that he was to take his tithe to church, he did an obvious and very moving thing. He counted up how much money he usually made in a year, divided by the days in a year, and arrived at a certain amount for each day. Then he took a tenth of that and put that much extra in his pocket every day. Then he went about his turquoise dealing with this daily earnest prayer on his mind: "Dear Lord, who needs this tenth of my money today? Lead me to the right person and I'll give it to him." He was as good as his prayer and his word and it was a daily adventure that had him so thrilled he could hardly stand it! Not bad for a novice, eh?

And the one sitting on the throne said, "See, I am making all things new!"   Revelation 21:5a (TLB)

"Nothing is as beautiful as something that has been restored," Raylene, our guest said, as she stood looking at the outlandish old mirror we had just had restored and finally had the courage to hang over the mantel. Our house is filled with old, huge, *exceedingly* outlandish furniture, but *this* mirror can hold its own even so!

Several years ago when Doug and I came to that crisis time that many couples come to, we went the usual route of separation and sorrow. However, the Lord undertook an enormous restoration project and with unique and perfect timing put us as individuals and our marriage back together. We then set about seriously building a life together and making a home. We bought a big old rundown house that needed everything. We began to repair and restore, just like we were doing with our minds and emotions.

We bought big old cheap furniture and applied the same principle—repair and restore. We took trips together in the States and overseas and looked at and loved everything that anybody else had restored. I think it fair to say that half the travel industry is built on people visiting restored homes, ruins, paintings, and whole historical areas. Man sets about restoring something to its original glory. This whole attitude is one that enriches our lives in a thousand ways.

But God, in his infinite love, goes us one better. When he restores, he doesn't have for his goal the original glory. His goal is to make everything better than it ever was, or ever could be. He makes all things new.

Man in his best natural state is still imperfect, sinning man. But man saved and restored can be a new man and a glorious saint.

A marriage in its best natural state is still filled with carnal pride and strife. But a marriage that has gone through the fire and had the water of God's love quench the fire and wash it clean has the capacity to be a resting place and a healing place, for the couple themselves and for other people as well.

There truly is nothing "as beautiful as something that has been restored."

And God is the Master Restorer.

And this is the will of God, that I should not lose even one of all those he has given me, but that I should raise them to eternal life at the Last Day.   John 6:39 (TLB)

Buz said, "I got so I could tell, when I started down that long lane and looked at the old house, if the furnace was out. The house would look cold." We laughed at him but he had a pretty good record.

They were faced with a monumental task, those newlyweds. We moved out and they moved in. It became their first home. The old house called "The Grove" was a two-story frame colonial, built just before the 1800s. The house was just like a grand old lady with arthritis; everything *would* work, but there was always a lot of creaking and groaning and a few false starts before the old joints would finally get going. Buz's brother Sarge and three close friends moved in to try to fill up the space, and Karen, the new wife, became an instant house-mother for four boys, plus a husband, a big dog, and a few cats. Buz became the caretaker of thirteen rooms and six acres. The pipes froze and burst, sending a spray of water into both kitchen and bath. Several trees came down in an ice storm, termites got a start, the water heater went out, and the lane alternately got so icy or so muddy they would have to hike in.

But the worst trial of all was always and forever the furnace. So with constant care and concern, Buz developed a sixth sense that told him when trouble awaited. He could "see the cold."

It made me remember when Karen was a tiny baby. She was premature and sick a lot of the time. She needed constant care. I could hear her cry and miss everything else. One time a building was being knocked down near us with one of those big swinging balls. I had dropped off to sleep on a downstairs couch and when the men started working in the morning, I slept on. But when Karen cried her small cry from an upstairs room, I was awake instantly. My senses were keyed to her slightest noise.

We somehow sensitize ourselves to those things that are important to us, those areas of responsibility where we feel we dare not fail.

My prayer, therefore, is to be so sensitized to those around that I will be able to "see the cold" in hearts and eyes and hear the small cries for help. For I believe that Jesus gives each of us people that we are responsible for bringing ultimately into his presence, just as he himself felt responsible to God for all those who were given to him.

RECIPES

It is possible to give away and become richer! It is also possible to hold on too tightly and lose everything. Yes, the liberal man shall be rich! By watering others, he waters himself. Proverbs 11:24-25 (TLB)

This is a little spiritual principle that is easy and second nature for some Christians and extremely gritty for others.

For Polly, my mother-in-law, it is extremely easy. She is naturally generous to a fault. She is also a wonderful cook. As a pastor's wife, through the years she has cooked and served thousands of scrumptious meals. She has collected recipes from ladies all over the world. Being a neat and tidy person, she copied all of them carefully and filed them logically.

This is no small accomplishment. My recipe box and many others I've seen look like scrambled eggs in a metal box. As a special wedding gift for our second daughter, Karen, Polly laboriously copied all her special recipes and gave them to her.

In a year or so Polly and PaPa Dale made a move and her own recipe box was never seen again. It was packed in a box with some valuable things, left in the station wagon, and they assume the whole box was stolen. She loudly lamented the loss of a lifetime of collected recipes. It was some time before any of us remembered that indeed they were not all lost—for Karen had a copy of all the *very best*. So, you see, she saved only the ones she gave away!

I press toward the mark for the prize of the high calling of
God in Christ Jesus.   Philippians 3:14

My father-in-law, Dr. Dale Oldham, tells this story:

During the Korean War, while attending a World Congress
on Evangelism, in Tokyo, I stayed with missionaries Nathan
and Ann Smith in the suburb of Tachikawa, just a block from
the large American Air Force Base.

At the close of the Congress, Nathan and I boarded a train
for a day of leisure at a R. and R. hotel located near the foot of
Mt. Fujiyama. For once the cloud collar generally seen covering
the upper reaches of Fujisan lifted, so that the snow-capped
peak shone forth in all its glory. It was very beautiful.

The train back to Tachikawa was well filled with Japanese
who had been climbing the well-worn mountain trail. Nearly
every climber held a staff in his hand—a staff marked every ten
inches or so with a special circle. Nathan, who had climbed
Fuji one time, said that there were way stations along the trail,
each manned by a Japanese attendant. As a climber reached a
station the attendant would stamp an indelible mark at the
proper place on his staff.

As we rode home I noticed with what pride each climber
held his stick. Some had gone only as high as the first or
second station. Others had gone up the mountain to the third,
fourth, or fifth stations. One or two had persevered and made

111

it clear to the peak, where a special mark of victory was stamped at the very top of their staffs. How proudly such staves were held! Later they would be displayed in living rooms where they would become centers of lively conversations with visitors.

The apostle Paul said that he pressed toward the mark of his high calling in Christ Jesus.

Let us also press on. Though we may have to pause now and then to get our strength, let not one of us give up the struggle until we reach the final way station and see our staff stamped with victory!

HIGH NOON

And when he came to himself, he said, How many hired servants of my father's have bread enough and to spare, and I perish with hunger! I will arise and go to my father, and will say unto him, Father, I have sinned against heaven, and before thee, And am no more worthy to be called thy son: make me as one of thy hired servants. And he arose, and came to his father.

Luke 15:17-20a (NAVES)

The time when a person "comes to himself" and is born again is like a time of high noon on a brilliant, sunny day. Things appear just as they are at high noon. There are no shadows falling on either side to alter their true appearance. There is, likewise, no moonlight to lead the mind to fanciful imaginings. Our view of ourselves and our own lives is for the first time one of a perfect viewing. The shadows are forever after altered.

Before high noon in our lives, the shadows point to the going down of the sun, to the west—to the vanishing of our day, when the night will reign forever. After high noon they point back again to the east—to the eternal rising of the Son, and his entrance through the eastern gate! The Bible says there will be no night there, for the Son is the light.

So we do not ever again look forward to an eternal night time. We forever look forward—and our shadow points—to the rising of the Son!

A LIVING LIKENESS

King Herod soon heard about Jesus, for his miracles were talked about everywhere. The king thought Jesus was John the Baptist come back to life again. So the people were saying, "No wonder he can do such miracles." Others thought Jesus was Elijah the ancient prophet, now returned to life again; still others claimed he was a new prophet like the great ones of the past.

"No," Herod said, "it is John, the man I beheaded. He has come back from the dead." Mark 6:14-16 (TLB)

There was something that they recognized, these men of old, there was a quality about Jesus that they had encountered in those other few men. They could not name it, but they could recognize it. This Jesus was a living likeness of those disturbing uncommon prophets of the past.

When our third little girl was a tiny baby, her grandmother, Polly, laughed and cried over a certain mannerism of this little child. It was peculiar to only one other person she had ever known, and that was her father-in-law, the child's great-grandfather. He had been gone for many years and yet here was something that was peculiar to him, showing up in his great-grandchild. A living likeness, because of the family bloodline.

So these contemporaries of Jesus struggled with defining what it was about him that arrested their hearts. We know the prophets were men chosen and used by God. We also know that Jesus was the Christ.

What seems like an impossible goal for the heart, but a worthy goal, is that we might have something about us that is a living likeness of him.

THE DOORWAY

"A curse on you, you hypocritical scribes and Pharisees! For you bolt the doors of the kingdom of heaven in men's faces, for you neither go in yourselves, nor do you let those who are trying to do so go in." Matthew 23:13 (Williams)

This was among the seven scathing truths that Jesus threw at the religious leaders, just before they decided he must be killed in order to save their precious positions of power and prestige. It is like bringing up the curtain and turning on the spotlight to a still vignette, so that all of a sudden, the audience understands the mystery. Many religious leaders, the ones chosen and given the task and opportunity of showing others that theirs is a spiritual life, are standing in the doorway, blocking the very door of heaven. They will not go in themselves, but to worsen the crime, with arms folded and proud looks, they bar the door, so others who would go in, cannot enter.

This electrifying view of how it really was sent Jesus to the cross.

It also reminds us that anyone claiming his name must be *inside* the spiritual door of heaven himself, and be welcoming others in, not blocking the doorway.

Jesus wants open doors, open hearts, welcoming arms to usher us into his kingdom.

*And may the Lord make your love to grow and overflow to
each other and to everyone else, just as our love does toward
you.*   I Thessalonians 3:12 (TLB)

My three-year-old granddaughter grabbed me and gave me a
big hug. Then with a look of iridescent love on her perfect little
cameo face she said, "Oh, Gramma, we're sweethearts, we
match!"

When I told my husband, her "Papa Dougie" about it, he
said, "I guess everybody wants somebody with whom to
match."

In big people's language the translation of "match" is "com-
patible." Lots of divorces are granted on the grounds of
incompatibility—always from someone who once was chosen to
be his sweetheart. Why? Because they matched!

I got to thinking about this business of matching. I didn't go
out into the world and look at all the babies available and
choose Jamaica. She came into my world and I love her just
because *she is.* She happens to be a beautiful, perfect child. But
the experience of other grandmothers assures me that if she
were not—if she were misshapen, or sickly or abnormal in
some way—my love would be the same, and if different, more
pure and intense.

She, likewise, didn't get the chance to go around and survey
all available grandmothers and choose the perfect one. She
loves me just because I am. When she grows up and sees the

116

imperfections, in all probability she will only laugh about them and still love me.

Therefore, loving and matching and compatibility can't be as hard as we make them. If we set our hearts to lavish love on "whomever" *is* in our lives, just like granddaughters and grandmothers lavish love on each other, most of our mis-matches would disappear.

Our society pays too much attention to *choosing* our love. Otherwise why would the most enduring and endearing bonds on earth—our children and grandchildren—be people we never get a chance to choose! They come to us unknown strangers. We pronounce them "God-given" and set about the business of loving them. Would that we give the same break to those matches in our lives that we choose!

And beyond all these things put on love, which is the perfect bond of unity.   Colossians 3:14 (NAS)

But the woman is the glory of the man.
I Corinthians 11:7b (NAS)

A virtuous woman is a crown to her husband.
Proverbs 12:4a (TLB)

The woman is the *glory* of the man! Is there any way to describe glory? It is stepping from darkness into many-faceted, all-encompassing light. It is having the veil lifted and suddenly being able to comprehend the beauty of all things as God originally planned. It is exhilaration! It is being able to know and sense the true spirit of God just as if a floodlight brought it all into focus. Glory is a touch of something beyond this world. It is fragrance. It is beauty. It is light. It is truth.

The Bible tells us glory comes from these sources:

1. It is given by the Lord God.

For Jehovah God is our Light and our Protector. He gives us grace and *glory*. No good thing will he withhold from those who walk along his paths.   Psalm 84:11 (TLB), italics mine

2. It is given by Jesus.

"I have given them the glory you gave me—the glorious unity of being one, as we are."   John 17:22 (TLB)

3. It comes through the work of the Holy Spirit.

But we Christians have no veil over our faces; we can be mirrors that brightly reflect the glory of the Lord. And as the Spirit of the Lord works within us, we become more and more like him.
II Corinthians 3:18 (TLB)

There is a great deal of talk today over women's rights. It is necessary, I suppose, in our world, but it wouldn't be—if we considered the perfect way. When the woman loves the man, as she ought, she serves so well that her work and achievements and ministrations take on a glint of glory, a word that is heavenly and "beyond our saying" in meaning.

I'm sure that is why we are so repulsed when a woman acts in a base manner. It is not meant to be so. And it is significant that the glory comes through her goodness, her hard work, her service, her thorough approach to life. This is confirmed in Proverbs 31:10.

Why should women settle for equal rights when what the Lord intends is that they should be "a glimpse of glory"!

 BURRS

Remember the old phrase from cowboy days, "a burr under the saddle," used to describe something that really irritated you?

Our little dog, Snugs, got into a patch of burrs and briars one day. They were knotted up tight against the skin, and had to be cut out. We thought it would be a real job to get them out, that Snugs would kick and fight through the whole process. Do you know what he did? He let me lay him on the floor, roll him on his back, and he lay as still as a toy dog, while I carefully clipped around each burr! Why? Exceedingly smart dog, apparently. He must have known those burrs were going to hurt him, not me, if we didn't get them out.

Now, if I can just learn to be as smart as our dog, I can ask my Master, the Lord Jesus, to cut out the burrs and irritations in my life—the ones that are really tight up against the skin. It's something I can't do for myself. It takes my Master's hand. The process is all tied up with two real basics—repentance and forgiveness. Those are the two parts of the Master's scissors.

Oh, to be burrless!

EARTHQUAKES

Even though they are immensely frightening for us as people, earthquakes make me smile at God. They're like a woman moving the furniture around in her house. She gets tired of it always looking the same old way. So she pushes and shoves and rearranges it to her satisfaction. Imagine being able to say, "I think I'll move that mountain and rearrange that river!"

Reel Foot Lake was formed out of just such a fit of house-cleaning by the Lord. It was formed by an earthquake. At the time of the earthquake there was such an upheaval that the mighty Mississippi River actually ran backward for a little while! The lake that was formed from that cataclysm is a natural phenomenon. It is a very clear, shallow lake with wonderful fishing, a real paradise for sportsmen. It is different in many ways from any other lake in the United States.

Is it any wonder that sometimes the Lord gives *us* a good shaking? He needs to form rich new deposits in our souls. He needs to swish the water around and make some new channels in our lives. It won't be quite so scary, the next time I get an earthquake in my life, if I remember he is probably just "cleaning house and rearranging the furniture." The result will be something new and wonderful—just like Reel Foot Lake!

Whereby are given unto us exceeding great and precious promises: that by these ye might be partakers of the divine nature, having escaped the corruption that is in the world through lust.   II Peter 1:4

And the glory which thou gavest me I have given them; that they may be one, even as we are one.   John 17:22

It was said of an old man that "his face was like an ancient chapel, with all the lamps inside lighted up for evening worship."

Doug had an experience that makes this quotation a reality. About a year before her death, he sat for a couple of hours one afternoon with Ethel Waters and talked with her. They were in her home. In the midst of the conversation about her life, she started to sing, just for him, the words to a Bill Gaither song:

"I'm going to live the way He wants me to live,
I'm going to give until there's just no more to give,
I'm going to love, love 'til there's just no more love,
I could never, never outlove the Lord."

He said it gave him goose bumps, for when she started to sing, it was like a light had been turned on inside and her face was aglow!

There is no other explanation for a phenomenon like this, other than the fact that it is the glory of the Lord, shining through like a lighted lamp, giving an old and wrinkled face the beauty of an ancient chapel.

And let him be drenched with the dew of heaven.
Daniel 4:15b (NAS)

Consider a drop of dew as it rests on the velvet petal of a rose. What is it like?

It is like a diamond. It is perfect, pure, full of light, a gift of God.

Who can destroy it?

If the wind shakes it from the rose and it falls to the ground, it only does what it was meant to do. It brings moisture to the earth which in turn brings condensation—which in turn brings dew.

Who can destroy a diamond?

A rock cutter can cut it into many pieces, yet each tiny piece is still a diamond. You spoke of yourself, Father, as the Living Water. If we drink deeply of you, we will thirst no more, for your Spirit, like the dew, and like its representative the diamond, cannot be destroyed.

THE TEMPLE

And I saw no temple therein: for the Lord God Almighty
and the Lamb are the temple of it.   *Revelation 21:22*

These words are part of John's revelation, spoken about the new Jerusalem, the Holy City, that came down from God out of heaven.

Our earthly need for a special *place* to worship God will cease to be. The one we have sought to honor and to worship with these special buildings will be there, and literally be the temple, personified. The Lord God Almighty and the Lamb *are* the temple.

All the tent tabernacles, the myriad of small, humble wooden churches, the magnificent abbeys and chapels of Europe, the beautiful Spanish missions, the thousands of spires all across our earth have been but a way for our worshiping spirits to walk, like stepping stones over water, bringing us closer and closer and ultimately into the glorious presence of the Almighty God and the Lamb, the true temple.

This is where our journey is leading us—into a glorious presence of him who was and is and ever shall be. The Alpha and the Omega.

The need for building is past. We will be with the Living Presence, the true temple!

Selah! which is to say, "Let it be so!"